The Turn of the Tide

Robert J. Rance

authorHOUSE®

AuthorHouse™
1663 Liberty Drive
Bloomington, IN 47403
www.authorhouse.com
Phone: 1-800-839-8640

First published by AuthorHouse 2/4/2011

ISBN: 978-1-4567-1742-1 (sc)
ISBN: 978-1-4567-1743-8 (e)
ISBN: 978-1-4567-1744-5 (hc)

Library of Congress Control Number: 2011902106

Printed in the United States of America

This book is printed on acid-free paper.

Cover Illustration by Franz Franc

Eileen Rance

Dedication

THIS BOOK IS DEDICATED TO EILEEN, MY loving wife of 55 years. While successfully raising our four children, she found the time to contribute in countless ways to the SOS project. Often Eileen worked well into the night preparing bulletins, press releases, and letters that were important to our campaign. Without her sacrifices throughout the sixteen years of our endeavor, we might not have been successful.

Bob's determination to complete this book carried him through his final weeks. The manuscript was in production when he succumbed to cancer on August 28, 2010, in Miami, Florida.

Preface

THIS BOOK HAS BEEN WRITTEN FOR TODAY'S generation of striper anglers, wildlife and fishery authorities, conservationists, naturalists, biologists, and those who, like myself, treasure all the sea life our oceans provide.

For many years I have felt compelled to write about the "behind the scenes" political chicanery designed by those who sought to defeat management bills that would save the striped bass.

These events took place some 40 to 50 years ago and are presented to the best of my recollection and with supporting documents that are in my possession. I have done my best to recall the names of all those who were involved in the events.

In 1967, Irwin Levy, Blair Moger and I, concerned about the possible extinction of the striped bass, formed an organization called SAVE OUR STRIPERS (SOS). What began with a handful of members eventually became an organization composed of individual and club memberships which, at the height of our campaign, numbered an estimated 87,000 strong. SOS became a force to be reckoned with.

In 1984, fifteen years after our efforts to set a new minimum possession size of 24 inches for the striped bass had begun, the bill was signed into law in New York State. It had been through some rewrites and changes, but we were happy to have won a victory for the striped bass that would, we hoped, ensure its existence.

This could not have been accomplished without the many members and volunteers who gave selflessly of their time and effort.

I also wish to express my gratitude to New York Assemblyman Patrick Halpin for his sponsorship and effective campaign to gain passage of the SOS bill. Without his full commitment we would not have succeeded. Also, thanks to the New York Sportsmen's Federation for suggesting that we seek Assemblyman Halpin's sponsorship.

Contents

Please see the appendix for samples of the letter writing campaigns that covered almost two decades. They were selected from hundreds of documents concerning the striped bass management bill and the PCB concerns in fish.

Chapter 1
My Addiction

IT WAS TUESDAY EVENING AND MY OFFICE clock showed 5:30. I snatched up my briefcase and headed for Penn Station to board the 5:59 train for Long Island. It would take me to my home and family in Massapequa Park, an incorporated village on the south shore about 40 miles out of New York City. Leaving the office this late would ensure me a seat for the long ride. My commute usually took an hour and a half door to door.

Eileen, my wife of twenty years, greeted me with a kiss. She informed me that she had already fed our four starving kids and my dinner was waiting. I pulled off my tie and sat down to a fast meal.

Glancing anxiously at my watch, I calculated that I had just 25 minutes to hit the road in my beach buggy. I gulped down the rest of my meal and quickly pulled on my fishing clothes. If all went well, I should be arriving at the inlet beach in time to catch the turn of the tide.

My fishing buddies and others would already be on the small outer bar from which their hooks could reach predator fish feeding in the deeper fast-running current. If I arrived too late, there might be no room for me on the narrow sand spit. As I crossed the waist-deep slough in the dark, I could just make out the human forms already gathered on the bar. I quickly found a casting spot in the middle of the line of anglers, noting that two rods were already bent with fish on.

Snapping a blue and white darter to my line, I held my cast until no one else was casting, then fired my two-ounce lure up-current at about a 45-degree angle. I reeled in the slack line as the fast current carried my lure past me. Then, as my line tightened, the plug began to throb enticingly. I reeled more slowly and got a good strike. I tried to set the hook but missed. Then another strike followed, and another. Before the action died, I had taken two bluefish and released a feisty, undersized striped bass that was hardly longer than my lure. Another angler not far from me landed a twelve-pound striper, while others loaded up with bluefish.

The slough that I had crossed earlier was now reduced to a mere trickle. With rod on my shoulder and fish on a stringer, I trudged my way up the dune to my beach buggy. I removed my headlamp, waist belt, plug bag, and waders. Several swallows of the still-hot coffee from my Thermos quickly revived me. It was now past one in the morning. By the time I got home, gutted and iced down my fish, it would be three o'clock before I could join my tolerant spouse in a warm, comfortable bed.

I set the alarm for 7:15 a.m. and rolled into bed, planning to catch the 8:12 into the city. When the fish were present in the surf, this would be my routine two or three times a week. It was an addiction that would rule my life for years. Catching the turn of the tide became my master.

Chapter 2
Good Friends and Cold Nights

EARLY ON IN MY FISHING DAYS I met Frank Keating, a former police reporter turned fishing columnist. Frank suggested that I would benefit from membership in the High Hill Stripers, a surf fishing club with about 30 members. They held monthly meetings and competitions and knew the ins and outs of catching the big ones. Little did I know that his suggestion would have a tremendous impact on the next fifteen or so years of my life.

Some of the members spent weekends at Montauk State Park, the striped bass capital of the East Coast. Keating described these fishermen as both knowledgeable and competitive; in his words, they were true sportsmen. Taking his advice, I became a member and began spending weekends and vacation days with them.

Montauk's growing popularity with anglers was due to the size and abundance of the catches from these waters. The Point jutted out into Block Island Sound and the game fish had to pass its shores as they migrated south from Cape Cod, New England, and Long Island Sound to warmer waters. They also were in hot pursuit of the south-moving forage fish such as herring, anchovy, sand eels, mullet, and squid.

To make my frequent trips to the Point, I purchased a Volkswagen camper and equipped it with oversized tires, which I deflated to increase traction on the sandy beaches. It wasn't much to look at, but it was comfortable and dependable. Most important, it provided protection and warmth from harsh winds when the weather was foul.

It was on just such a blustery night that I headed out to Montauk Point to join my fellow surf rats at the North Bar, a usually productive game fish location. My considerate wife stopped me as I was leaving and handed me a bottle of Southern Comfort.

"Here," she said. "This is to ward off any chills."

Normally the drive took about two and a half hours, but on this night I was anxious to get there and catch the outgoing tide. I passed the paved parking lot and glanced up at the old brick lighthouse, now painted red and white. The structure had been commissioned by President George Washington in 1792. It had stood, since its completion in 1796, as a beacon to warn ships of the treacherous rocky shoals that surrounded it. The Montauk lighthouse was New York's first, and was a popular destination for history buffs.

I continued down the deeply rutted track to the North Bar where I hoped some of my buddies were also crazy enough to show up on such a night. I angled the VW up close to three other buggies parked there and hastily suited up. I donned heavy waist-high waders, a foul-weather jacket, an old army belt from which hung a hand gaff, fish chain, and a sheathed knife. My headlamp dangled from my neck as I picked up my surf rod and started walking. We had discovered that if we placed our headlamps on our heads, other fishermen could spot any possible action. Some even sat in their buggies watching through binoculars to see who might be having luck; but, with the lamps hung around our necks, any light beams were hidden by our bodies from the shore.

As I waded carefully into the windblown surf, I struggled to keep my balance on the slippery boulders with the butt end of my surf rod. I could see that those already out there were being buffeted by the pounding waves. After less than a half hour of this punishment, all of us were soaked and frozen. We headed back to our vehicles.

My buggy was in a position that offered the most protection from the stinging northwest wind and we gathered on its lee side. Remembering the bottle of Southern Comfort that Eileen had handed me when I left home, I suggested we get in the buggy.

"I've got something that will warm us up a bit," I said. "Let's get in out of the cold."

The five of us squeezed into the camper and I produced the bottle. We passed it around, each of us taking a good, healthy swallow. The smooth liquid both warmed us and improved our mood. We began swapping fish stories and experiences. As the bottle made the second round our tongues became looser and the stories better. We were passing the bottle for the third time when someone suggested we get back to the water.

We gathered our gear and, in the best of moods, hastened a bit unsteadily toward the bar. But now the small slippery boulders, that had been submerged in hip-deep water, were completely exposed. We had missed the outgoing tide and any fish that had been present!

Rance, (far left) and High Hill Striper Club buddies shield themselves from wind behind his VW buggy.

Chapter 3
The Big One

THE YEAR WAS 1964 AND I HAD been with the High Hill Striper Club for about a dozen years. The members were diverse in many ways except one, and that was their collective enthusiasm for, and dedication to, the sport of surf fishing. This was the club's last contest of the year.

I awoke in the bone-chilling cold. It was mid-November and although I was fully dressed, right down to two pairs of heavy socks, the thin blankets I had brought provided little protection against the low 40-degree temperature. Now partly awake, I saw by the light of my flashlight that it was only two o'clock in the morning.

My three fishing buddies and I planned to awaken about 3:30 a.m. to catch the turn of the tide under the lighthouse. Late straggling striped bass in the fall migration were our goal. Pulling myself into a ball to preserve my body heat, I soon drifted back to sleep, only to be awakened by Fred banging on the window of my VW.

"It's three-thirty. Get up," Fred Schwab yelled, as he hurried across the parking lot.

Muttering under my breath and feeling insane for

pursuing a sport that makes such harsh demands on one's body, I struggled out of the back of the buggy and pulled on my waders, my jacket, my army belt with all of its paraphernalia; hung my headlamp around my neck, grabbed my surf rod from the roof rack, locked the buggy, and hurried to catch up with my companions.

Fred and Al Rees had already exited the parking lot and were crossing the highway to a footpath that wound through thickets down to the rocks below the lighthouse. As I reached the edge of the bluff, the eerie sweeping beam from the lighthouse revealed a number of anglers already occupying the choice rocks far out in the surf. From there they could cast into the incoming current. Just before I started my descent to the shore below, I hastily reached for my plug bag to select a lure.

"My bag! Where is it?" I shouted to myself. I ran my hands around my waist again but it wasn't there. "You idiot," I said, retracing my steps up to the parking lot. There, next to the buggy, was the bag of lures. I snatched it up and some fifteen minutes later was down at the shore. I waded out and began to search for a perch from which to fish. The best rocks were taken so I had to settle for one small, flat rock that sloped slightly backward. Adjacent to it I found a small rounded boulder for my left foot. Together they would require some delicate balancing, particularly whenever an incoming wave broke around my legs.

Waiting, I watched as Al cast up-current, reeled in the slack in his line and settled to a slow retrieve. This allowed his plug to do its job of enticing a strike from any nearby stripers. Meanwhile, an angler on my left cranked

8

his plug halfway in. I took this opportunity to haul back on my eleven-and-a-half-foot fiberglass rod and fired my yellow darter plug up-current as all of the anglers on the point were doing. If this procedure were not followed by all of us, a terrible tangle of crossed lines could result. Still another threat existed in the waters below, should a fisherman allow his lure to settle to the bottom. The entire area was strewn with glacial boulders, large and small, to which were attached long, inches-wide strands of leathery, tough, brown seaweed. Hooking into these could cause still more tangled lines and the possible loss of a lure. I felt somewhat protected against this latter danger because of the brand new 20-pound test monofilament line I had spooled on my surf reel just for this trip.

Al called over, "Any strikes?"

I responded with a "No, not yet. You?"

"No," he shot back.

Just as the lighthouse beam passed overhead, I thought I saw an angler far out on a large rock land and release a small striper. Some fifteen minutes elapsed and by this time the incoming current was ripping past the Point. It was then that I spotted a good bend in Al's rod. He skillfully fought a good-sized striper past the boulders, dismounted from his rock, and beached his catch on the dry, rocky shore behind us.

I followed and we pulled out a scale to weigh his trophy. It read 26 pounds. I slapped Al on the back.

"You have this contest all sewed up," I assured him. While envious, I was nevertheless happy for his catch. This was our last opportunity to win something in the club's final competition of the year.

I waited for several large waves to break and wash in before wading back out to my rocks. The wind out of the north began to pick up. My wet hands were freezing, making it difficult to keep a firm grip on my rod and reel. Some relief was provided, however, by the occasional wave that splashed the warmer-than-air water over my hands.

Perhaps some ten or fifteen minutes had passed when my pulsing lure somewhere out in the dark came to a stop. My line tightened. I immediately pulled back on my rod several times to set the lure's treble hooks. In response, an unstoppable force began to peel yards of monofilament off my reel. Al saw the struggle and yelled encouragement. The increasing wind whipped around the Point, making my taut line sing like an out-of-tune harp string.

What I assumed to be a large striped bass ran an estimated 60 to 70 yards before slowing, at which point I began to alternately pump and reel to turn it in my direction. Reluctantly it began to give ground and started to follow my lead. About two-thirds of the way in, the striper must have brushed against a boulder or some seaweed and realized that it was in shallow water. This threat energized the creature and it took off on another run for deeper water.

I was awed by the strength of this cow bass. I knew it was a cow because most stripers weighing more than fifteen pounds are females; the males of the species seldom exceed that weight. I turned her on the second run and carefully worked her in between the rocks in front of me.

In the dark she had veered to my right and had broken the surface with a loud slap of her broad tail, almost scaring an angler off his perch.

"What the f--- was that?" he yelled.

Al shouted back, "Bob has a big fish on."

He hurried to shore to leave his rod, then came back out to help gaff my fish. I led the tired female to him. Just as he swung the gaff hook, a breaking wave crested with the fish on top of it. Al's gaff bounced harmlessly off the striper's scale-armored back. Startled, she again charged toward deeper water, this time for a much shorter distance. Al yelled out to me, "Bob, it looks like a 40-pounder. Be careful."

If this were true, it would be my biggest striper ever. Now, thoroughly whipped, the big cow easily let me place her in front of Al and his gaff. But again, a large wave crested just as Al took deadly aim. The wave completely engulfed both Al and the fish. Only his hand, gripping the gaff, which was this time hooked firmly in the striper's back, was visible.

For a moment I feared for my friend's safety. Then Al shot up, sputtering, the water streaking off his eyeglasses which miraculously he had not lost. Grinning triumphantly, he dragged my prize out of the wash onto the shore. I was in close pursuit. Together we pulled the cow into the shelter of a small cranny in the rocky bluff to get a better look at her. When I saw the actual length and girth of my catch, I was overwhelmed. At first the experience of this big catch was exhilarating. Then the enormity of the thing sank in and I was in a state of shock. My prize still had the yellow darter crosswise in her mouth, much like a dog with a large bone. I bent over to try to work the hooks free and the lure simply fell out. Just how lucky can a fisherman get!

Other anglers who had witnessed the fight gathered around for a look. After a number of estimates as to her weight, someone pulled out a Chatillon scale, the surf angler's old standby. With the help of several friends, we lifted the fish high enough for the large hook to hold it. The scale bottomed out at its 50-pound limit, which meant that we would need a bigger scale. Several club members recommended that we try to get the fish weighed at Kronuck's tackle store, a favorite hangout for Montauk's visiting surf fishermen. I draped the heavy fish over my left shoulder and started up the path to the parking lot, but could only make it a few feet. Ritchie Huebner saw my struggle and kindly offered to go up to the lot and bring down his army Jeep to carry the fish to the top. We propped its heavy body over the right front fender. I climbed in and held the fish through its gill plate while Ritchie drove up the bluff to the parking lot.

As we passed Artie Glass's beach buggy, Fred rapped on his windows and shouted out to him, "Look at Bob's 50-plus-pound fish!"

Artie, only half awake, muttered, "Oh yeah?" and resumed his nap.

It would be a number of hours before Johnny Kronuch could be rousted out of bed. Since it was still dark, we decided to drive down to North Bar, where another group of our club members had been fishing the outgoing tide. We were eager to show off the fish, but word had already reached them about my lucky catch. Al Kaich happened to have a color-film camera with him and asked me to pose for some shots.

Three hours later, as the sun was rising, Fred, Al, and I drove into Montauk and banged on the door of the tackle shop. We knew Johnny Kronuch was closing for the winter season and would be heading for Florida this very day.

Finally, a light came on in the back room and a figure came stumbling to the front. Without opening the door, Johnny yelled, "What do you want? I'm closed."

"We want to weigh a fish," we shouted in unison as Al held up his 26 pounder for Johnny to see through the window.

"That little rat! You woke me up to weigh that little rat?" Then, with some colorful language, he told us to get lost.

With that, I dragged my trophy into view. The door unlocked quickly and Johnny shouted, "Now that's a fish!"

Kronuch took his official balance scale down from the rafters where he had stored it for the winter and hung it up from a large eye bolt that was screwed into a ceiling beam. We lifted the big bass onto the hook under the scale. Johnny slid the balance weight to a point that was level. My fish weighed 58 pounds and 13 ounces. The grizzled surf fishing veteran pronounced my catch the largest striped bass ever landed and weighed on the East

End of Long Island. Montauk was, and still is, considered the striped bass capital of the northeast. He recommended that I have it mounted and gave me the name and address of a top taxidermist in Florida.

The landing of this record-breaking fish was the high point of my long angling career. It also marked another turn of the tide and started me on a long journey of another kind, a journey that was to prove significantly more meaningful.

Bob with his record setting striper.

Robert with record catch striper, 50" long, 58lbs
13oz.- caught under Montauk Point Lighthouse.

Chapter 4
Fish and Fame Almost Lost

TWO WEEKS HAD PASSED SINCE MY RECORD catch. Johnny Kronuch recommended that I have taxidermist Al Pflueger in Hollywood, Florida, mount it. I made arrangements with a Pflueger representative in Queens to put my trophy in deep freeze for several weeks prior to shipping it by refrigerated Railway Express car to ensure its safe arrival.

One night as I sat at the dining room table, I looked through the doorway at the spot on the living room wall where my trophy would be displayed. I had selected this strategic location so that no visitor to our home would fail to see it. Then there was the added advantage of the picture window in the living room where, if anyone passing by on the sidewalk chose to sneak a peek, they would not be disappointed.

My head was filled with visions of my importance among the High Hill anglers. I confess I also realized and enjoyed the touch of envy I knew many of them would feel.

I envisioned approaching tackle manufacturers to lend

17

them my trophy for displays at sporting goods conventions and shows. This would give me even greater fame. But a telephone call that day from Pflueger started a series of events that quickly knocked me off my lofty pedestal.

The taxidermist was calling from Florida to find out when the fish would be shipped so he could prepare for its arrival. I wondered why he had not contacted his tackle store agent directly, but told him I would find out the answer and get back to him that day.

It was a long drive to Queens from Massapequa Park, but I managed to arrive while it was still daylight. As I approached, I saw that the store's interior was dark. Alarmed, I tried the door. It was locked. Then I spied a notice from the county stating that the store was in bankruptcy!

There was no explanation, no telephone number, nothing. My head and shoulders slumped as I envisioned the power off and my fish thawing and rotting—both my fish and my fame gone.

"Robert," I said to myself aloud, "thy name is hubris."

What should I do? What could I do? I suddenly remembered Jim Ketchum, a lieutenant with the Nassau County Police Department and a respected member of High Hill Stripers. I dashed home and put in a call to him.

"Let me do a little investigating and see what I can find out," Jim said. "I'll get back to you as soon as I know something." Later that night Jim called and gave me the good news.

"Your fish is safe; the freezer is operating. Only the interior lights were turned off to keep customers away. Here's the number you need to get hold of the owner."

"Wheew! I can't thank you enough, Jim," I said. "I'll call right now."

Chapter 5
The Arrival

TODAY WAS THE DAY! MY FISH WAS to be delivered by Railway Express. Sure enough, when I got home from the office, the huge wooden crate was sitting in the middle of the living room. Eileen had set out wine glasses, a bottle of wine, and a bottle of cola for the kids to celebrate the big event.

I threw down my briefcase and raced for the garage to retrieve a hammer and screw driver. My son, Bob Jr., helped me remove the corrugated cover from the front of the box. There was my fish in exactly the pose that I had requested. I loosened the screws that held the fish to the crate and, with Eileen's help, carefully lifted it out to hang on the wall. I had measured countless times to make certain my prize would fit in this spot. When it was exactly as I had pictured it should be, we filled our glasses and made a toast!

During the Christmas holidays I took a hiatus from fishing and spent some time putting my gear in order for the next season. As I poked through my bag, my hand grasped the yellow darter that I had landed my striper with. It was a gift from Al Rees and was superior to any other manufactured plug that I had used. He had designed it of heavier wood to cast further and run deeper in the Montauk rip current without losing any of its action. He also equipped it with larger and stronger hooks and suggested that I attach a heavy leader about twenty feet long which would enable the lure to settle deep in the water, reducing its chances of catching on the long, leathery seaweed that was so abundant. While it might mean losing an occasional lure, I would not be so apt to become entangled with other anglers' lures. Al's lure had served me well.

Robert with three of his children (left to right), Donna, Judy, and Bob Jr. in 1960.

Chris and his dad with stripers 31 lbs and 34 lbs.

Bob Jr. proudly displaying his catch

Chapter 6
Problems for the Stripers

WITH THE HOLIDAYS BEHIND US, THE HIGH Hill Stripers began their regular meetings and activities. But now problems other than catching fish for sport were becoming topics of conversation.

New York State received daily reports on estimated recreational catches of striped bass by anglers, and actual catches by the commercial fleets. These reports, known as "green sheets," were noting a 40-percent drop in landings.

It was then, in 1967, that Irwin Levy, Blair Moger, and I decided to form an organization dedicated to the preservation of the striper. One of our High Hill Stripers, Artie Glass, came up with the name SOS for Save Our Stripers. The members took to it immediately.

A major issue, as we saw it, was the commercial fishing industry, comprised of haul-seiners and gill netters. These fishermen took an estimated 80 percent of the daily catch of stripers during their fall migration.

Then there was the problem of the nuclear power plant. It had been common knowledge for some time that

Consolidated Edison Power Company had not yet found a way to keep fish from going through the turbines that rushed cooling water to the nuclear furnaces at Indian Point. If the fish did manage to get through the turbines without being chopped up, then they were killed by the super-hot, scalding water that came from the nuclear furnaces.

Blair Moger was an elementary school teacher in Sayville. He saw these problems as an excellent opportunity to educate his students about the need to be "custodians of the environment." He began teaching them about the problems that the stripers were having, and even tested students on the related lessons. In addition, he thought this was a good way to get their parents involved.

I was deeply concerned about still another problem. As an avid reader of science and environmental journals, I began to come across articles warning about the high levels of mercury and polychlorinated biphenyls (PCBs) that were being found in diets, particularly those that included fish. For years my family had been eating the fish I caught on a regular basis. My catches supplemented our weekly meals, making it financially possible to raise four kids. Now I was learning that it may have been harming all of us.

Years later, my wife and I, and two of our four children were diagnosed with cancer. A radiology-oncologist expressed his opinion that all the cancer cases in our family were the result of our diet.

It was a devastating statement and I thought of not just my family, but all of my fishing companions and their families who, like myself, had been catching and eating contaminated fish. This indestructible man-made chemical was used in countless products, including transformer coolants, plastics, paints, and toys. In fact, PCBs could be found in almost any item one could name. Dioxin, a byproduct of PCB, was particularly harmful to humans, and was declared a probable carcinogen by the federal government.

A federal clearing judge had been appointed to decide what levels of PCBs would be safe to consume. The clearing judge determined that the level of PCBs in fish and other seafood should be lowered from five parts per million to two parts per million. This ruling was to be instituted within 90 days. During this time frame members of the public would be allowed to voice their opinions for or against the ruling.

Tony Taormina, Director of the New York State Marine Division, was placed in charge of the sampling for PCBs for the state. There seemed to be little concern about some of the samples that were taken, even though they had high levels of PCBs.

One particular striper sample taken from the Montauk area contained 21 parts per million of PCBs, but Taormina said he did not consider it typical of the Montauk area and excluded it from the report. The commercial fishermen insisted that the contaminated fish were not coming from the Montauk area, but from the Hudson River area.

I caught a large striper off Fire Island and sent off a sample of it to be tested for PCBs. The tissues contained fourteen parts per million of the contaminant. I immediately wrote to Taormina and charged him with biased sampling.

Disgusted with the foot-dragging and disregard for health as well as for the environment, I began a letter-writing campaign against the deadly PCBs and their byproduct, Dioxin.

I wrote to President Jimmy Carter, to Vice President Walter Mondale, and other key officials in Congress and in the state government. I hoped they would be concerned about the delays.

I submitted the letters to the board of directors of SOS for their review. After receiving their approval, I mailed the letters not only to government and health officials, but also to the media. That included newspapers, radio and television stations, the Associated Press, and other news entities.

The letters had immediate results. The U. S. Food and Drug Administration (FDA) was bombarded with inquiries as to why the clearing judge's ruling had not been instituted. The FDA immediately issued an order for compliance and appointed a temporary commissioner to handle the problem. This commissioner, it was expected, would be assigned the task on a fulltime basis.

The public was again given 90 days to voice their opinions, pro and con. At the end of that period, the ruling appeared in the Federal Register, a daily report of activities on government rulings. Finally, the two parts per million in fish and other seafood was established as the standard to be adhered to, but it had taken eight years.

Chapter 7

Invitation to a Lawsuit

SOS WAS NOW BEING RECOGNIZED AS AN important voice for the saltwater and Hudson River striped bass. As president of SOS, I was contacted by lawyers from the Natural Resource Defense Council (NRDC). This dedicated group later became an international organization.

They asked if SOS would consider joining the Hudson River Fishermen's Association as co-interveners in a suit against Consolidated Edison Power Company. The suit was for damages that Con-Ed's nuclear power plant at Indian Point was causing to the striped bass and other fish. This location was an important spawning and nursery area for many valuable species.

The Association was concerned about the intake of Hudson River water needed to cool the extreme heat from the nuclear furnaces. They knew it was taking its toll on the fish as well as the plankton on which the fingerlings depended for food.

We were aware of Con-Ed's attempts to solve the problem with screens to prevent the fish and plankton from flowing through the turbines. They had also employed loud underwater percussion devices and high-frequency noises that were intended to frighten away the immature fish. But so far nothing had been successful.

SOS held a special meeting to vote on participating in the lawsuit. Clearly the members felt the project was worthwhile, but our concern was the initial outlay of funds to cover the cost of filing the suit. The amount needed was more than half the total in our treasury.

We agreed to join in the lawsuit, but told the environmental lawyers we could not afford any other fees or payments beyond the initial outlay for the court filing. We decided to raise more cash by raffling off items contributed by tackle companies and other interested fishing organizations at monthly and annual fishing tournaments. We also said we would arrange to have information booths at various tackle equipment trade shows throughout the Atlantic Coast states to increase membership.

Six lawsuits later, the Hudson River Fishermen's Association and the Save Our Stripers were declared victorious. Con-Ed was required to retrofit its cooling towers to accommodate greater amounts of cooling water. It was also forced to build a much larger cooling pond that was close-cycled and no longer drew water from the Hudson.

This victory made clear the necessity of employing a riverkeeper, a person whose task it would be to oversee the waste that companies had, for years, been dumping into the Hudson River from Albany all the way to Indian Point.

The riverkeeper's task was to take regular samples of the waste discharges from commercial establishments along that stretch of the river and monitor the condition of the water.

John Cronin, a former commercial fisherman, was appointed official riverkeeper and was provided with a special craft equipped to sample the waste discharges. He found that no one was measuring the amount of radioactive materials flowing into the river. Nor were toxic cleaning fluids that were used periodically to scrub down the cooling towers being measured. Cronin notified General Electric that there was proof the company was spilling contaminants into the Hudson. Although the victory over Con-Ed had been a major step toward cleaning up the river, clearly much more work remained to be done.

Chapter 8
Dirty Deals

IT WAS NOW ALMOST 1984, SIXTEEN LONG years after SOS had begun its crusade to save the striper. The years of endless meetings, telephone calls, long nights at the typewriter drafting press releases and bulletins were drawing to a close. The bill was to be debated soon. My wife, Eileen, who had been my right hand throughout the years, always supportive, and I, could now turn our attention to other matters.

I could not help but feel a certain guilt over the burden I had placed on my family while I gave so much effort to this campaign. Although there was a great sense of pride that we had accomplished so much, I also felt a sadness for the many obstacles SOS and I, personally, had encountered. I recalled the rancor and subterfuge that seemed endemic to the political system. The obvious bartering for favors, not to mention the greed that kept the wheels turning, were clear evidence that our victory would have to be won again and again.

I remembered, for instance, a certain city council member who, after a meeting, called me aside and, in hushed tones, promised he could get the council to put its full support behind the bill. When I gave him a questioning look, he nodded reassuringly and asked, "How much money do you have?"

I was stunned and realized that I was seeing a very seamy side of politics, one that I had only read about in newspapers. I was embarrassed and shaken by his brazen solicitation for money. I mumbled that I would have to get back to him and quickly left. Of course, I never responded to his proposition. The city council later voted to support the bill, without the tainted councilman's help.

During an SOS meeting I reported, for the sixth or seventh time, that the Majority Assembly Speaker Perry Duryea was continuing to use assembly rules and parliamentary procedure to bottle up the bill in En-Con Committees or on the floor of the assembly. After many attempts, I finally got a brief meeting with Duryea to discuss negotiations. His behavior nurtured a love-hate relationship in me because, although I despised his greed, I was impressed with his ability to use the rules to his advantage. He was clearly a worthy opponent.

Duryea agreed to a meeting but insisted it be held at the ice house he owned and operated. He also insisted that commercial fishermen be present, ready to show several of us a map of the area where the fishermen were willing to give up setting their nets. However, they came to the meeting without a map.

Clearly Duryea had a conflict of interest with his lobster business, ice house, and his purchases of striped bass from the commercial fishermen for resale to markets and restaurants. Although some of the fishing columnists drew attention to his activities, nothing was ever officially addressed.

After an SOS meeting at which I had again reported on Majority Assembly Speaker Perry Duryea's continued resistance, an enthusiastic young volunteer invited me, not for the first time, to go fishing with him some night at an old, broken-down pier area where he told me he caught a lot of stripers. I explained to him that I couldn't, because I had early commutes into the city every morning on the Long Island railroad.

He must have realized that I wondered about his motives, because he drew closer and, in a half-whisper, said, "I'm connected. Do we want to make a hit on Duryea?"

I knew he was not kidding. He lived in Little Italy over a restaurant frequented by family members. I quickly assured him there was no need for such action.

Reporters wrote of death threats made to Duryea. Once a newspaper was left on his desk. Inside the smelly package was a dead striper.

But the ugliness came from both sides. Early in our campaign to get the bill passed, our first sponsor, a nursery grower who evidently had not read the bill thoroughly, got a phone call telling him he should drop the sponsorship. He was told it would ruin the commercial fishing industry and put people out of work. After he too received a newspaper-wrapped fish, he withdrew his support.

Chapter 9

"One Man Against the Survival of a Species"

AS AN ADVERTISING SALES AND MARKETING EXECUTIVE with Hearst Corporation, I had many interesting clients. Martin Landey, president of a Madison Avenue advertising agency, was one of them. Coincidentally, he also was an avid fisherman.

One day when we were enjoying lunch together, he related the story of a fishing trip that had been ruined by commercial netters. It seems that while he was fishing from his Donzi for stripers at the legally-required distance from the rock jetty, commercial netters surrounded him with their net in order to land as many fish as they could. When he objected, they threatened him with a shotgun they had on board, supposedly to keep sharks at bay. He had been furious, but could do nothing.

It so happened that Landey and Ray Petersen, who was publisher of Good Housekeeping magazine and my big boss, as well as an executive director for Hearst Corporation, were best friends and neighbors. They commuted together each day into the city, and both knew of my passion for the striped bass bill that I had worked on for so long. Apparently they had discussed it many times.

Now, as we were having lunch, Landey suggested that he might be able to help out with the campaign.

"Bob, I'd like to run an ad in The New York Times about your bill."

"That would be much appreciated, Martin," I replied, thinking perhaps he had a small space left over from another ad campaign. "But I don't want the members of SOS to run into any legal problems."

"Let my copy writers work together with my lawyers to come up with a solution that will protect the SOS members. I'll try to get it in the paper this week," Landey said.

Several days later, as I walked out the front door, I scooped up the paper and headed the block and a half to the Long Island railroad station. That day I was catching the late train so I was pretty much assured a seat. Sure enough, I found a spot next to the window. With no one beside me, I placed my briefcase on the seat and opened the Times. I scanned the headlines, then began flipping through the pages.

There, in bold relief and filling an entire page, were the words "ONE MAN AGAINST THE SURVIVAL OF A SPECIES." The rest of the text referred to Perry Duryea, who was known in the state assembly as "The Silver Fox." The ad implied that blame for the near-demise of the striped bass could be placed directly at the feet of the Assembly Majority Speaker. It was simply signed, "The Ad Hoc Committee." I was overjoyed! The ad went a long way toward swaying opinion in favor of the bill.

One man against the survival of a species.

In the New York State Legislature last year, a bill was presented that would have prevented the striped bass from becoming our country's next "buffalo."

The gamefish bill would have protected striped bass from what is called commercial seine fishing (a kind of indiscriminate mass killing of millions of striped bass every year, no matter what their size).

The bill was approved (54 to 1) by the Senate of this State.

But one man stood in its way.

One man pocketed the bill so it couldn't reach the Assembly floor, where the people's voice through their elected officials could have been heard.

One man named Duryea.

A conflict of interest, maybe?

It so happens that as well as being an Assemblyman representing commercial fishermen, Mr. Duryea also has commercial fishing interests.

We ask: should one man be allowed to pocket a bill that 54 State Senators (representing you) said they wanted passed?

We ask: should one man be able to decide the possible life or death of a species?

After all, this bill we are asking for is not so revolutionary. Already, in New Jersey, Connecticut, Massachusetts, New Hampshire, Maine and along much of this magnificent sea coast of ours, it is illegal to commercial seine fish for striped bass.

Now this bill (A-1550) has been reintroduced by Mr. McCarthy and multi-sponsored by Messrs. Thorp, Burns, Jerabek, Reilly, Balletta, McCloskey, Biondo, Pisani, Flack, Michaels, Straub, Kremer, Harwood, Wager, Schmidt, Cooperman, Berle, and Harris.

The bill makes sense to anyone who loves the sea and its creatures, to anyone who loves what is left unspoiled of nature.

(The way we keep attacking this land and sea of ours, it's getting so the only way you will be able to see anything that belongs to nature is by going to a zoo, an aquarium or a museum.)

We ask for your help.

Now, we know that all of you are not vitally concerned in particular with striped bass.

But we do think you might be concerned with the survival of a species. We do think you might care enough to at least fill out this coupon and mail it.

If you do, you will help us keep our bill out of Mr. Duryea's "pocket" and help us get it into the hands of your elected representatives.

And if that happens, you will not only help millions of striped bass, but all the people who want to see nature, and nature's own, survive.

(3)

39

Chapter 10
On Camera with Connie Chung

THE CONGRESS WAS BEGINNING TO TAKE NOTE of the striper problem and created a committee to research various sides of the issue. Our SOS bill went through several amendments in the assembly, and although it gave some ground, it managed to hold onto its support. Assemblyman Patrick Halpin was firmly committed to the bill and spoke eloquently and often for its passage.

The SOS bill was scheduled to be reported, out of committee, to the senate floor for a vote. However, the chairman of the En-Con senate committee failed to present it. Instead, he held our bill back to work on a weaker version of his own bill.

Fred Schwab and I learned what he had done and went straight to the office of the Senate Majority Whip Steve Bianchi, to advise him of the chairman's actions.

Without a word, Bianchi grabbed the telephone, dialed the chairman, and cursed and sputtered into his ear.

"I thought I told you to report that bill yesterday," he screamed. Then Bianchi shouted, "Now get that damn bill to the floor for a full vote."

Fred and I looked at each other and smiled. We had crossed another hurdle.

Then another bit of good luck came our way when NBC called and asked if I would appear on a news show to talk about the striper bill. This interview occurred a few days before the big debate between Assemblyman Halpin and representatives of the commercial fishermen.

We arranged to meet Connie Chung and her crew at Robert Moses beach. Cameras rolled as several SOS members suited up in gear as if preparing to surf fish. When the cameras turned to Chung holding a microphone, she began by asking me to explain the bill and what SOS was trying to accomplish. We talked about the research that determined a striper should not be landed unless it was at least 26 ½ inches. At that size most females would have had at least one season to spawn, thus giving the species an opportunity to procreate and, hopefully, survive.

Chung did an excellent job with the interview and I was pleased that the bill had received such good coverage, both from the full-page ad in The New York Times that Martin Landey had arranged, and from the national TV coverage on NBC.

Chapter 11
The Big Debate

FINALLY THE DAY OF THE BIG DEBATE in Albany arrived. The chamber was packed. Assemblyman Halpin, our bill's sponsor, and the opposition were ready for the fight. The commercial fishermen were well-represented.

I was there in the balcony, my chin hanging over the railing, straining to catch every word. With me were Bob Buss, the current SOS president, Fred Schwab, and Fred Hodgson.

Someone later remarked that they could not remember an environmental debate that had lasted so long. Assemblyman Halpin spoke with conviction as he painted a picture of the Atlantic coast migratory pattern without the striped bass. It was a convincing argument and the bill we had worked on for so many years was passed at last, by an overwhelming majority. In 1984, Governor Mario Cuomo signed the bill into law.

As I said when I began this narrative, I have stated the facts as I remember them. Others have written about these events from their perspectives and I offer no quarrel with them. I only wish to add my own observations and experiences. The years have somehow accumulated, a little faster than I might have wished. No doubt some details have been forgotten, but of one thing I am certain. I have not forgotten the energy, the persistence, and the devotion that so many gave to help preserve this small part of nature. I consider the time well spent.

It is my fervent hope that others will take up the sword and continue fighting for the preservation of all sea life, and against the exploitation and pollution of our planet for personal gain.

Assemblyman Patrick Halpin, New York,
speaks out on striper legislation.

"To Bob Rance-

*Without your commitment to the Striped Bass
we would have never gotten this far*

Pat Halpin"

Robert, (far right) with fellow SOS members
present award to the honorable Joseph Pisani for
his commitment to fishery conservation.

Robert J. Rance

August, 2010

Miami, Florida

Appendix

Box 116
Massapequa Park, N.Y. 11762

Bulletin No. 13   November 1970

DURYEA TACTICS PERPETUATE STRIPER SLAUGHTER

Unnecessary waste of an important sportfish as commercial fishermen load
truck with striped bass. Note useless kill of non-marketable "trash fish"
that were trapped in the net and will end up littering the shore.

For the majority of you who fished New York waters this year, 1970 has been a poor
season for striped bass. We suspect that even the commercial catch may be down. To
learn more about the striper problem and what you can do about it, read further.
. . . and please remember to fill in and mail the membership form on the back page.

BOYCOTT MONTAUK

HELP MAKE STRIPED BASS
A GAMEFISH

SUPPORT THE THOUSANDS OF SPORTSMEN
WHO REFUSE TO BE INTIMIDATED BY
ASSEMBLYMAN PERRY B. DURYEA
AND HIS MONTAUK BUSINESS ASSOCIATES.

DON'T SPEND MONEY
IN MONTAUK.

SPREAD THE WORD.

FOR INFORMATION, WRITE:
SAVE OUR STRIPERS, BOX 116, MASSAPEQUA PARK, N.Y. 11762

S AVE **O** UR **S** TRIPERS INC. BOX 116, MASSAPEQUA PARK, N.Y. 11762

SOS

Bulletin No. 46   October 1983

WE DID IT!

BUT NOT WITHOUT HELP

Governor Cuomo

he 24-Inch

tricter rules enacted

...riped bass angler

Nice going, Mario!

limit

omo

...uomo up...

...andard

...striped b

Minimum Size

...Striped Bas...

...by St...

GOVE

SIGNS STRIPER BILL

INTO LAW

Striped bass law

signed by Gov

53

SAVE OUR STRIPERS, INC.
Box 116
Massapequa Pk., L.I., N.Y. 11762

May 28, 1977

Hearing Clerk
Food & Drug Administration
Room 4-65, 5600
Fishers Lane
Rockville, Md. 20857

Dear Sir:

This statement is submitted by Save Our Stripers, Inc. in connection with the Administration's announcement in the Federal Register of April 1, 1977 of its proposal to reduce the temporary tolerance levels of PCBs in several classes of foods. Our remarks are specifically directed to the proposal of lowering the tolerance level of PCBs in fish, from the present 5 parts per million to 2 ppm.

Our organization has reviewed the testimony and evidence presented in the printed report of the proceedings of the National Conference on Polychlorinated Biphenyls held in Chicago, Illinois, November 1975. In addition, representatives of SOS have attended several state and federal hearings on the subject.

If the animal test results studied by the Food & Drug Administration are accurate, and if the standards used for arriving at toxic levels of PCBs in fish are similar to standards used to determine toxic levels in other classes of foods, then Save Our Stripers concurs that for the safety and protection of the fish-eating public, the new lower tolerance level must be imposed.

It is noted that page 17492 of the April 1st Federal Register, under the heading of "PCBs In Fish", carries the statements, "Anadromous species had relatively high PCB levels, the highest in whole fish being 17 ppm (Striped bass caught in the New Jersey area). However, the average levels in these species were less than 3 ppm in whole fish and less than 0.5 ppm in edible portions." It is evident that at the time of publication of your announcement, your agency was not aware of the existence of a striped bass from Long Island, N.Y. waters, the edible flesh of which revealed a high PCB concentration of 21.53 ppm. This, and still others with relatively high levels, were analyzed by the Marine and Coastal Resource Division of the New York State Dept. of Environmental Conservation. For your review, we are enclosing copies of correspondence from the Division, plus two lists of Long Island striped bass samples which the Division tested for PCBs. Please note that while the lists

were said to be complete, a subsequent newspaper article revealed the purposeful omission of at least one specimen caught in the Montauk Point area of Long Island that tested out at 8.89 ppm. The same Newsday article (attached) also quotes the Division director as saying that the samples were not random but were taken from selected areas which, ". . . we thought would be polluted."

It is our organization's opinion that such select sampling and the purposeful omission of one sample with a high reading is biased research and ignores the fact that the striped bass is migratory. Therefore, we have added the Montauk Point striped bass with the 8.89 ppm concentration to the enclosed lists. It should also be noted that the mean average concentration for these 66 samples, most of which represented edible portions of the striped bass, well exceeds 3 ppm.

The same Division director and another state official are reported to have proposed that PCB-contaminated fish be treated in the same manner as cigarette packages, that is, that they carry a warning against consuming too much fish. Just how they propose to print a warning label on fresh, unprocessed fish, or on a broiled fillet of striped bass in a restaurant, is beyond our comprehension. If they are serious, we consider such a plan to be dangerous and totally unacceptable. For example, it is known that when a cigarette smoker stops smoking for a certain number of years, his lungs regain their original pink color, and his system rids itself of the toxic substances. However, it is our understanding that such is not the case with PCBs, which remain in the adipose tissues and certain body organs indefinitely. Additionally, the proposed warning would offer little protection to the uninformed, the illiterate, the pregnant, the nursing infant, juveniles and the unborn. It is for these reasons that SOS is unalterably opposed to the idea of simply warning the public.

Emotional charges are being made by a small, but vocal group of commercial fishermen and their local representatives from Eastern Long Island, that if the 2 ppm tolerance level for fish is imposed, (1) they will be deprived of their livelihoods; (2) the recreational fishery will be seriously hurt; and (3) the public will suffer. Sampling indicates that a new lower tolerance level of 2 ppm would affect the sale and consumption of only three species of fish in the New York area. These would be the common eel, the striped bass and the bluefish. Statistics will show that the eel represents only an insignificant percentage of the total seafood consumption in New York and in the United States, and therefore of little loss to the market fishermen. A ban on the sale of striped bass would likewise cause only moderate hardship to the netters. The species can only be harvested about six months of the year, and represents but one portion of their total season's catch. It is obvious that for these reasons, the netting of striped bass is only part time, and provides only a supplemental source of income. Aside from this, the striped bass is a relatively unimportant fish commodity, representing less than one half of one percent of all the seafood marketed nationally.

Should striped bass, and possibly bluefish, be affected by the new, safer PCB level, it would not put commercial fishermen out of business. There are at least ten other edible fish species available for harvesting in the New York area.

We do not accept the argument that the recreational fishery will be seriously hurt. Undoubtedly, there will be a temporary period of adjustment while sport anglers become accustomed to the idea of releasing their contaminated striped bass or bluefish, instead of bringing them home. We are convinced that any possible losses to Eastern Long Island charterboats, motels, and gasoline retailers will be negligible and of short duration. Sportfishermen bent on fishing will not give it up simply because they may not be able to keep their catch. Many already release their striped bass as a conservation measure.

As to the loss to the public, they would be least affected by a change in the safety level in fish. There are many other kinds of excellent saltwater fish available for them to choose from at the market, many of them less expensive than striped bass. The removal of striped bass from the dinner table will cause no major hardship for consumers.

Instead of directing their attacks against the Food & Drug Administration, whose responsibility it is to protect the public from toxic and dangerous substances in foods, drugs and other consumer products, the commercial fishing group and their representatives should be criticizing the polluters and the state agencies that knowingly permitted the Hudson River to become a waste receptacle for toxic PCBs.

Under no circumstances should the health and safety of the public be compromised, nor the peddling of poisoned fish be tolerated, simply to protect the supplemental income of a small group of part-time market fishermen.

Very truly yours,

Robert J. Rance

Robert J. Rance, President
57 Glengariff Road
Massapequa Park, N.Y. 11762

RJR/er

(516) 541-8676

GENERAL⟩ ↔ PCB'S Are A
ELECTRIC⟩ National Problem

The recent dumping of PCB's along 210 miles of North Carolian's highways has focused attention on these toxic substances. Estimates of the cleanup cost in North Carolina run into millions of dollars, but officials admit that any estimate is still a rough guess. The three New York men charged with dumping the chemicals are being indicted under seven criminal charges in North Carolina, with a possible maximum sentence of 42½ years in prison for each man. Federal indictments could add another eight years to each man's sentence. Although the environmental effects of the spill are yet unknown, the North Carolina Wildlife Resources Commission is just one of the State agencies monitoring the situation. The Commission has been studying PCB concentrations in doves, rabbits, and fish in the immediate area of the spill.

North Carolina is not the only state grappling with PCB problems. According to the National Wildlife Federation, New York and Michigan also have large-scale PCB problems.

The State of New York is now asking the federal government for $25 million to clean up the PCB pollution in the Hudson River. PCB contamination in the Hudson River and in the Chesapeake Bay in mid-Atlantic region has been earmarked as one of the causes of the decline in striped bass population along the east coast. The Chesapeake Bay, and to a lesser degree, the Hudson River, are the two prime nurseries for the Atlantic Coast population of striped bass.

PCB's are also a problem in the Great Lakes. The State of Michigan recently warned fishermen not to eat more than a half-pound of salmon per week caught out of Lake Michigan and Huron, due to high PCB concentrations in the fish.

There's also some good news. The Environmental Protection Agency has proposed a ban on the manufacture, use, and importation of PCB's. These highly toxic chemicals are used primarily as insulating fluid in electrical equipment. The ban would be effective this January 1, if passed. A voluntary ban has been in effect in this country since last year. According to the EPA, more than a billion pounds of PCB's have been used by American industry since 1929, and approximately 440 million pounds of the toxic chemical are now loose somewhere in our environment.

January 1979 (B.F.N.) BASS FISHING NEWS

S AVE O UR S TRIPERS INC.

P.O. BOX 116

MASSAPEQUA PARK, N. Y. 11762

February 8, 1979

Commissioner Donald Kennedy
U.S. Food & Drug Administration
14-81   H - F - 1
5600 Fishers Lane
Rockville, Md.   20857

Dear Commissioner Kennedy:

SAVE OUR STRIPERS is an organization with a membership of
8,700 sport fishermen, and is supported by the majority of New
York State's 250,000 recreational striped bass anglers. We are
writing to protest the unreasonable and unwarranted delay in
announcing the new tolerance level of 2 parts per million for
PCBs (polychlorinated biphenyls) in edible fish. Your agency
had previously concluded that such a step is necessary. Yet,
according to a front page article in the January 2, 1979 New
York Times, pressure from certain state officials, state agencies
and some commercial fishing lobbies has apparently persuaded the
Food and Drug Administration not to act.

Since the announcement in the Federal Register during April,
1977, our group has directed a number of telephone inquiries to
your office, only to be advised that, "the statements submitted
by interested parties are still being reviewed". 21 months have
elapsed since the original announcement in the Federal Register.
In the meantime, new and more incriminating evidence of the PCB
danger has come to the attention of your staff.

According to the Times article, your agency admits that a
new allowable level of 2 ppm. would eliminate a "relatively minor
percentage of marine fish and less than 25 percent of freshwater
fish from commercial markets". In light of this, your delay in
establishing the new tolerance level makes no sense.

If, as was suggested, your agency is concerned about the
economic impact of such a move, we remind you that your Department's regulations to ban fluorocarbons from aerosol sprays,
cyclamates from dietetic foods and beverages, and DDT from in-
secticides, had far greater economic implications. Yet this did
not deter your agency from acting to guard the public's health.

SAVE OUR STRIPERS, INC.

PCBs' threat to the many unsuspecting victims ingesting contaminated fish is real, and it is unconscionable for a protective government agency to take the position that it must weigh a loss of profits on one hand, against possible cancer, liver damage, birth defects, reproductive problems, and nerve disorders, on the other.

We urge that you set the new lower tolerance level for PCBs in fish without further delay.

Very truly yours,

Robert J. Rance
Exec. Vice President

RJR/er

cc: Pres. James E. Carter
Sen. Jacob K. Javits
Sen. Daniel Patrick Moynihan
Rep. Jerome A. Ambro
Rep. Thomas J. Downey
Rep. Norman F. Lent
Mr. Richard Severo, N. Y. Times

DEPARTMENT OF HEALTH, EDUCATION, AND WELFARE
PUBLIC HEALTH SERVICE
FOOD AND DRUG ADMINISTRATION
WASHINGTON, D.C. 20204

December 18, 1979

Mr. Robert Rance
57 Glengariff Road
Massapequa Park, NY. 11762

Dear Mr. Rance: P79-29888

This is in response to your letter of November 16, 1979 requesting the
Federal Register document stating the PCB tolerances for fish.

We are enclosing a copy of the June 29, 1979 Federal Register which is
the final rule for PCB's reduction of tolerances. We are also enclosing
a copy of the October 5, 1979 Federal Register, PCB's - Reduction of
Tolerances Confirmation of Effective Date and Partial Stay.

Sincerely yours,

Rosalia H. White

Rosalia H. White
Assistant to the Director
Division of Regulatory Guidance
Bureau of Foods

67

UNITED STATES ENVIRONMENTAL PROTECTION AGENCY
WASHINGTON, D.C. 20460

OFFICE OF PESTICIDES AND TOXIC SUBSTANCES

APR 8   1980

Mr. Robert J. Rance
Executive Vice President
Save Our Stripers, Incorporated
P.O. Box 116
Massapequa Park, New York   11762

Dear Mr. Rance:

I recently received a copy of your letter to Ms. Dorothy
Campbell, dated February 12, 1980, and I would like to respond to
your questions concerning Environmental Protection Agency (EPA)
policy regarding the possible interaction of various toxic
chemicals within the human body.

It is a well established fact that many chemicals act as co-
carcinogens, or may be toxic only when metabolized. For example,
although some chemicals themselves may not be specifically toxic,
they may be metabolized to extremely toxic end products. Such is
the case for nitrates, which are metabolized to nitrosamines.
Some chemicals may be carcinogenic only in the presence of a
second chemical or their carcinogenicity may be greatly increased
by the presence of a second chemical, such as is the case for
asbestos and cigarette smoke and hence they are co-carcinogens.
Furthermore, extremely toxic contaminants may be present as trace
contaminants of other toxic or non-toxic chemicals. For example,
polychlorinated dibenzofurans (PCDF) are generally found as
contaminants in polychlorinated biphenyls (PCBs).

For the purposes of regulation, however, it is not necessary to
determine whether a particular chemical or its metabolic end
product is the "bad actor." To limit the risks associated with
environmental and human exposure to the metabolite necessitates
the regulation of the chemical itself. The same logic may not
hold true for trace contaminants which might be removed in
separate processes. To be effective as regulators we must focus
on the primary agents.

69

We are concerned with mechanisms and reactions that cause the
final toxic reactions, chronic or otherwise. EPA laboratories do
research these mechanisms. I must point out, however, that EPA
is not a major center of this type of research. Rather, we rely
heavily on information from the more traditional medical research
community in academia and government.

I trust this response is helpful to you. Please feel free to
contact me again should you need additional information.

Sincerely,

John P. DeKany
Deputy Assistant Administrator
 for Chemical Control

DEPARTMENT OF HEALTH, EDUCATION, AND WELFARE
PUBLIC HEALTH SERVICE
FOOD AND DRUG ADMINISTRATION
WASHINGTON, D.C. 20204

September 30, 1980

Robert J. Rance, President
Save Our Stripers Inc.
P. O. Box 116
Massapequa Park, NY 11762

Dear Mr. Rance:

This is in response to your letter of September 15, 1980, regarding the status
of the stayed 2 parts per million (ppm) tolerance for polychlorinated biphenyls
(PCB's) in fish.

The agency has not yet determined whether or not an administrative hearing is
warranted. The objections to the 2 ppm tolerance are still being evaluated. I
have enclosed a copy of the October 5, 1979 Federal Register notice that
announced the stay in case it contains any information you do not already have.

We appreciate your concern that the decision on the hearing has not yet been
made, however, we are evaluating the pertinent information as expeditiously as
our limited resources permit. The agency's decision will be announced in the
Federal Register as soon as practicable.

If we can be of further service, please let us know.

Sincerely yours,

Elizabeth J Campbell

Elizabeth J. Campbell
Guidelines and Compliance
 Research Branch
Division of Regulatory Guidance
Bureau of Foods

Enclosure

SAVE **O**UR **S**TRIPERS INC.

P.O. BOX 116

MASSAPEQUA PARK, N. Y. 11762

March 8, 1982

Dr. Arthur Hayes, Commissioner
U.S. Food & Drug Administration - 14-81
H. F. I.
5600 Fishers Lane
Rockville, MD 20857

Dear Commissioner Hayes:

SAVE OUR STRIPERS is a sport-conservation organization with a combined membership of 8,000 covering nine states. Since the early seventies, S.O.S. has been concerned about, and involved in actions to safeguard the public from the dangers of polychlorinated biphenyls (PCBs).

In 1979 we applauded your agency's declaration of safer lower levels of cancer-producing PCBs in milk, poultry, eggs, and edible fish. At that time, a 2 parts per million tolerance level for PCBs in fish was announced in the Federal Register, and the public was offered an opportunity to comment on the new levels. Apparently, there was little opposition to the lower levels proposed for milk, poultry and eggs. However, we understand that certain commercial fishing industry interests did object to the 2 ppm level proposed for edible fish, on economic grounds. On October 5, 1979, the final regulation for fish was stayed. It is extremely difficult to understand why it has taken 2½ years for the F.D.A. to review and study the evidence that had been presented by the commercial fishing group. Our latest information tells us that the "hearing judge" has at last presented his recommendation to you to help you decide whether the new 2 ppm guideline for fish should stand.

SAVE OUR STRIPERS is concerned about the fish-eating public's unnecessarily long exposure to the toxic PCBs since 1979, and hopes that you can now bring this matter to a quick conclusion. We also hope that in arriving at your decision, you will wisely recognize that the public's daily exposure to the cumulative toxin is not limited to fish, or for that matter, to food alone. PCBs are in the air we breathe, the water we drink, and in many things we come in contact with. Fortunately, the Federal Government can provide some degree of protection by "outlawing" PCB-contaminated foods.

May we hear from you at your earliest opportunity.

Very truly yours,

Robert J. Rance
President

cc: Ms. Elizabeth Campbell

DEPARTMENT OF HEALTH & HUMAN SERVICES   Public Health Service

_____

                                              Food and Drug Administration
                                              Washington DC 20204
                    3 1 MAR 1982

Robert J. Rance
President
Save Our Stripers Inc.
P. O. Box 116
Massapequa Park, New York 11762

Dear Mr. Rance:

This is in response to your letter of March 8 to Commissioner Hayes about
the reduction of the PCB in fish tolerance.

Rather than respond to the substance of your letter at this time, we will
place your letter in the administrative record as a post-hearing brief.
(See enclosed Federal Register notice (47 FR 10079)). Your letter will,
thereby, be given full consideration in the Commissioner's decision
regarding the 2 ppm tolerance.

If we can be of further service, please let us know.

                              Sincerely yours,

                              Betty Campbell

                              Elizabeth J. Campbell
                              Assistant to the Director
                              Division of Regulatory Guidance
                              Bureau of Foods

Enclosure

S.O.S.
SAVE OUR STRIPERS INC.

P.O. BOX 116

MASSAPEQUA PARK, N.Y. 11762
(516) 541-8676

April 11, 1982

Dockets Management Branch
(HFA - 305)
Food and Drug Administration
Room 4 - 62
5600 Fishers Lane
Rockville, MD 20857

RE: Docket No. 77N-0080

Please send me a copy of the Initial Decision of the

Administrative Law Judge, announced February 2, 1982, on

Polychlorinated Biphenyls (PCB's) in Fish and Shellfish;

Reduction of Tolerances. Kindly mail to my home address,

below.

Very truly yours,

Robert J. Rance, Pres.

57 Glengariff Road
Massapequa Park, N.Y.
11762

79

SAVE **O**UR **S**TRIPERS INC.

P.O. BOX 116

MASSAPEQUA PARK, N. Y. 11762

June 7, 1982

Mr. Gerald H. Deighton
Director
Freedom of Information Staff
Dept. of Health and Human Services
Food and Drug Administration
Rockville, MD 20857

Dear Mr. Deighton:

On April 11, 1982, I wrote the Dockets Management Branch, requesting a copy of Docket #77N-0080. On April 26, I received a form letter response from you, advising that the requested record would be sent at an "early date".

It is now June 7, and I have yet to receive a copy of the record. I believe the "early date" to which you referred, must have passed by now.

If Docket #77N-0080 is not in print yet, could you please give me a better time frame in which to expect it. Would you kindly respond to the address below my name. Thank you.

Very truly yours,

Robert J. Rance, President
57 Glengariff Road
Massapequa Park, NY 11762

(Tel.) (516) 541-8676

S<small>AVE</small> O<small>UR</small> S<small>TRIPERS</small> <small>INC.</small>

P.O. BOX 116

MASSAPEQUA PARK, N. Y. 11762

(516) 541-8676

February 23, 1984

Dr. Mark Novitch
Acting Commissioner
U. S. Food & Drug Administration
5600 Fishers Lane
Rockville, MD 20857

Dear Commissioner Novitch:

It is with great concern that we are writing to you regarding the current "temporary" safe tolerance level of 5.0 parts per million for PCBs (polychlorinated biphenyls) in fish and shellfish for human consumption. These dangerous toxins cause tumors, neurological dysfunction, liver damage, still births, and birth defects in animals, and are listed as suspected human carcinogens by the International Agency for Research on Cancer.

It should also be noted that Canada adopted a level of 2.0 parts per million as early as November 1975. Ironically, that country has been shipping to the United States, PCB-contaminated fish that is unacceptable by Canada's own standards.

On April 1, 1977 the Food and Drug Administration announced in the Federal Register its intention to lower the tolerance levels for PCBs in dairy products, fowl, eggs, and fish and shellfish. This step was taken as a result of new information indicating that the chemical was more toxic to humans than was originally estimated. It was proposed that the level for fish and shellfish be reduced from 5.0 parts per million to 2.0 ppm.

That was almost seven years ago!

Since that time, arguments by objecting parties regarding the proposed regulation were submitted to your agency and reviewed. On October 5, 1979 the regulation pertaining to fish and shellfish was stayed, pending a determination of whether a hearing should be held on the question of your agency's estimate of the anticipated food loss that would

83

result from the reduced tolerance level. In the meantime, the lower tolerance levels for PCBs in dairy products, fowl, and eggs went into effect.

As you know, the disagreement between your agency and the objecting parties regarding the amount of food loss that would result, eventually went before an administrative law judge. His initial decision was handed down on February 8, 1982.

That last action should have cleared the way for a final decision by the Commissioner of the Food and Drug Administration — but it did not! As of this date, February 23, 1984, a decision has yet to be reached by your agency on whether the new tolerance level for fish and shellfish should be reduced to 2.0 ppm.

SEVEN YEARS OF INDECISION HAS SUBJECTED A HAPLESS FISH-EATING PUBLIC TO AVERAGE PCB LEVELS IN FISH OF UP TO 5.0 PARTS PER MILLION, WHILE, ACCORDING TO ANOTHER FDA REGULATION, ANIMALS ARE PROTECTED BY AN ESTABLISHED LEVEL OF 0.2 PARTS PER MILLION IN FINISHED ANIMAL FEED!

What is going on?

Is this yet another case of Federal agencies protecting big business at any cost, and "letting the public be damned"?

Very truly yours,

Robert J. Rance
Executive Vice President

RJR/er

cc: Sen. Howard Baker
    Sen. Patrick Moynihan
    Sen. Alphonse D'Amato
    Sen. Ted Kennedy
    Rep. Norman Lent
    Rep. Thomas Downey
    Rep. Guy Molinari
    Rep. Richard Ottinger
    Rep. Mario Biaggi
    Rep. Raymond McGrath
    Rep. James Scheuer
    Rep. Robert Mrazek
    Rep. Steve Solarz
    Rep. Claudine Schneider
    New York State -
    Gov. Mario Cuomo
    Com. of Health David Axelrod
    Com. of Environmental Consv.
    Henry Williams

Mr. Lane W. Adam,
    Amer. Cancer Soc.
Mr. James Siegel,
    Cancer Research Inst.
Dr. Ahmed Karim, Natural
    Resources Defense Council
Dr. Joseph Highland,
    Environmental Defense Fund
ABC-TV Network News
CBS-TV Network News
NBC-TV Network News
The New York Times
USA Today
The Daily News
The New York Post
Newsday
The Long Island Fisherman

S AVE O UR S TRIPERS INC. BOX 116, MASSAPEQUA PARK, N.Y. 11762

NORMAN F. LENT
4TH DISTRICT, NEW YORK

COMMITTEE ON ENERGY
AND COMMERCE

SUBCOMMITTEE:
COMMERCE, TRANSPORTATION,
AND TOURISM

COMMITTEE ON
MERCHANT MARINE AND
FISHERIES

SUBCOMMITTEES:
PANAMA CANAL AND OUTER
CONTINENTAL SHELF

COAST GUARD AND NAVIGATION

Congress of the United States
House of Representatives
Washington, D.C. 20515

PLEASE ADDRESS REPLIES TO THE
WASHINGTON, D.C. OFFICE
UNLESS OTHERWISE INDICATED

WASHINGTON OFFICE:
2228 RAYBURN HOUSE OFFICE BUILDING
TELEPHONE: (202) 225-7896

DISTRICT OFFICES:
☐ BALDWIN PLAZA BUILDING
ROOM 300, 2280 GRAND AVENUE
BALDWIN, NEW YORK 11510
TELEPHONE: (516) 223-1616

☐ MASSAPEQUA PARK VILLAGE HALL
151 FRONT STREET
MASSAPEQUA PARK, NEW YORK 11762
(516) 795-4454

February 29, 1984

Mr. Robert Rance
Executive Vice President
Save Our Stripers
P. O. Box 116
Massapequa Park, New York 11762

Dear Mr. Rance:

Thank you so much for taking the time to send me a copy of your letter to Dr. Mark Novitch, U.S. Food and Drug Administration.

I certainly share your concern over the levels of PCBs (polychlorinated biphenyls) in seafood for human consumption. In an effort to be of assistance to you in this matter, I am forwarding your letter to the Food and Drug Administration for further consideration and response. Please be assured, Mr. Rance, that I will contact you the moment I receive a reply.

Meantime, please feel free to communicate with me on any other federal matters of interest to you.

With best wishes I remain,

Sincerely,

NORMAN F. LENT
Member of Congress

NFL/ag

NORMAN F. LENT
4TH DISTRICT, NEW YORK

COMMITTEE ON ENERGY
AND COMMERCE

SUBCOMMITTEE:
COMMERCE, TRANSPORTATION,
AND TOURISM

COMMITTEE ON
MERCHANT MARINE AND
FISHERIES

SUBCOMMITTEES:
PANAMA CANAL AND OUTER
CONTINENTAL SHELF

COAST GUARD AND NAVIGATION

Congress of the United States
House of Representatives
Washington, D.C. 20515

PLEASE ADDRESS REPLIES TO THE
WASHINGTON, D.C. OFFICE
UNLESS OTHERWISE INDICATED

WASHINGTON OFFICE:
2228 RAYBURN HOUSE OFFICE BUILDING
TELEPHONE: (202) 225-7896

DISTRICT OFFICES:
☐   BALDWIN PLAZA BUILDING
ROOM 300, 2280 GRAND AVENUE
BALDWIN, NEW YORK 11510
TELEPHONE: (516) 223-1616

☐   MASSAPEQUA PARK VILLAGE HALL
151 FRONT STREET
MASSAPEQUA PARK, NEW YORK 11762
(516) 795-4454

March 13, 1984

Mr. Robert Rance
Executive Vice President
Save Our Stripers
P.O. Box 116
Massapequa Park, New York 11762

Dear Mr. Rance:

This is in further response to your letter expressing
concern over the levels of PCBs (Polychlorinated biphenyls)
in seafood.

Enclosed please find an interim reply which I have
received from Ms. Pamela Hackenberg, Department of Health
and Human Services. As you will note, your letter has
been referred to the Assistant Secretary for Health and
for reply. Please be assured, I will contact you the
moment I have anything further to report.

Meantime, feel free to communicate with me on any
other federal issues of interest to you.

With best wishes I remain,

Sincerely,

NORMAN F. LENT
Member of Congress

NFL/ag

89

G.E. to Pay for Striped-Bass Pollution

Special to The New York Times

RIVERHEAD, N.Y., Aug. 12 — Ending an eight-year fight, the General Electric Corporation has agreed to compensate New York commercial fishermen for income they lost because of PCB contamination of Hudson River spawning grounds for striped bass.

Under an agreement reached out of court Wednesday night, G.E. will pay up to a total of $7 million to 300 to 400 fishermen, including as many as 150 eastern Long Island baymen, who can prove they lost income as a result of a state ban on fishing for striped bass from 1986 to 1990 in marine waters off Long Island, and since 1976 in the Hudson River.

For 30 years until 1977, General Electric dumped PCB's into the Hudson, and only last month the company agreed to stem a new flow of PCB's into the river from a plant in Hudson Falls, 35 miles north of Albany.

The river is a major spawning ground for striped bass, a delicacy that once accounted for a large part of the yearly income for hundreds of commercial fishermen, including the dwindling number of full-time baymen on eastern Long Island plying a livelihood that dates from the Colonial period.

Lobster Pots or an Outboard

"It's become an ever more difficult task to live a life full-time on the water," said Arnold Leo, the secretary of the East Hampton Town Baymen's Association. "This money could help buy a new truck, or get some lobster pots or a new outboard motor."

The company said it agreed to the settlement in part because the legal action had lasted eight years and "would take at least another decade to conclude." The plaintiffs included

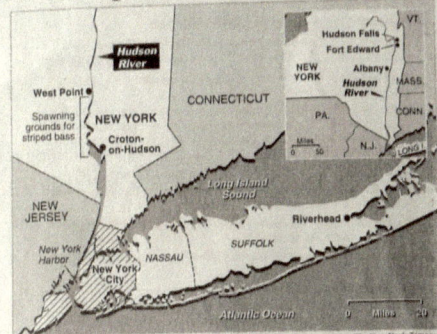

The New York Times

Until bans were imposed, commercial fishermen caught striped bass in the lower Hudson River and the waters off Long Island.

eastern Long Island baymen and fishermen from New York City and the Hudson Valley.

The company said it had agreed to create a fund of $7 million for claims made by the fishermen, which will be evaluated by a court-appointed neutral referee.

"Only those claimants who can demonstrate real economic loss will receive any money from the fund," G.E. said. There will be a cap on payments to individuals, the company said, but it did not give the amount.

Company Admits Little

A G.E. spokesman, Jack T. Batty, declined to disclose whether the company faced other PCB-related lawsuits or had entered into other settlements stemming from the dumping of PCB's into the Hudson River from the late 1940's until 1977, when the company voluntarily ceased the practice. He said the settlement did not mean the company was admitting that the PCB dumping may have caused damage to striped bass or lost income for the fishermen.

Congress banned the manufacture of PCBs, short for polychlorinated biphenyls, in 1978 after research showed that the chemical, which was used as an insulator in transformers, was highly toxic to fish and other animals.

The State Department of Environmental Conservation imposed a ban on commercial fishing for striped bass after amounts of PCB in the fish were found to exceed Federal limits, which were set at 5 parts per million in the late 1970's and lowered to 2 parts per million in 1986.

PCB, which is also a suspected carcinogen, was found to have accumulated in the fatty tissue of striped bass caught in the Hudson, New York Harbor and Long Island Sound and off the South Shore of Long Island. The fishermen say the chemical entered the fishes' food chain in the spawning grounds.

From Carolinas Northward

After spawning in Hudson riverbeds, the maturing striped bass swim south into the East River and into New York Harbor and east into Long Island Sound and the Atlantic Ocean. They range near the coastline from the Carolinas northward, and also spawn in large numbers in Chesapeake Bay.

Mr. Leo, of the East Hampton Baymen's Association, and several other

A $7 million fund to New York fishermen hurt by a PCB ban.

State Supreme Court here. The trial was to have begun on Aug. 19, but was postponed. The judge in the case, State Supreme Court Justice Mary Werner, must act on the settlement.

General Electric has said for years that PCB was discharged into the Hudson River from its plants in Hudson Falls and Fort Edward under permits granted by New York State.

In June, the owner of an industrial site in Albany, Vantrano Realty, sued G.E., complaining that a state-approved PCB cleanup plan the company is carrying out would fail to clean up the site. The suit is pending in State Supreme Court in Albany.

Settlement Cheers Baymen

News of the settlement bolstered the eastern Long Island baymen. They have bitterly complained that state regulations have sharply limited the number of striped bass commercial fishermen may take during the season from July to November.

"It's just crazy that we are allowed to harvest so few of them," said Mr. Leo, who objected to state regulations allowing sport fishermen to catch up to one fish a day from May to December. He said the commercial limit for the baymen was set at 46 fish each season despite the abundance of the fish in offshore waters this summer.

Gordon C. Colvin, the director of marine resources for the department, said the restrictions on eastern Long Island were part of a conservation effort agreed to by 13 East Coast states where stripers range.

"There is no question that there is a substantial increase in the number of striped bass going on right now," said Mr. Colvin. "But that is exactly what is intended by the cooperative management program the states have agreed to."

91

www.ingramcontent.com/pod-product-compliance
Lightning Source LLC
Chambersburg PA
CBHW030359290526
45785CB00004B/1825